Let's Explore

the Sun

Helen and David Orme

GARETH**STEVENS**

GS

PUBLISHING

A Member of the WRC Media Family of Companies

Please visit our Web site at: www.garethstevens.com
For a free color catalog describing Gareth Stevens Publishing's list
of high-quality books and multimedia programs, call
1-800-542-2595 (USA) or 1-800-387-3178 (Canada).
Gareth Stevens Publishing's fax: (414) 332-3567.

Library of Congress Cataloging-in-Publication Data

Orme, Helen.
    Let's explore the sun / Helen and David Orme.
        p. cm. — (Space launch!)
    Includes index.
    ISBN-13: 978-0-8368-7948-3 (lib. bdg.)
    ISBN-13: 978-0-8368-8133-2 (softcover)
    1. Sun—Juvenile literature. I. Orme, David, 1948 Mar. 1- II. Title.
    QB521.5.O76   2006
    523.7—dc22   2006034806

This North American edition first published in 2007 by
Gareth Stevens Publishing
A Member of the WRC Media Family of Companies
330 West Olive Street, Suite 100
Milwaukee, Wisconsin 53212 USA

This U.S. edition copyright © 2007 by Gareth Stevens, Inc. Original edition copyright © 2006 by ticktock Entertainment
Ltd. First published in Great Britain in 2006 by ticktock Media Ltd., Unit 2, Orchard Business Centre, North Farm Road,
Tunbridge Wells, Kent, TN2 3XF, United Kingdom.

The publishers would like to thank: Sandra Voss, Tim Bones, James Powell, Indexing Specialists (UK) Ltd.

ticktock project editor: Julia Adams
ticktock project designer: Emma Randall

Gareth Stevens Editorial Direction: Mark Sachner
Gareth Stevens Editors: Carol Ryback and Barbara Kiely Miller
Gareth Stevens Art Direction: Tammy West
Gareth Stevens Designer: Dave Kowalski
Gareth Stevens Production: Jessica Yanke and Robert Kraus

Photo credits (t=top, b=bottom, c=center, l=left, r=right, bg=background)
CArt Directors: 20; CORBIS: 21tr; NASA: 1all, 6bl, 7br, 10, 11bl, 17bc, 22bl, 23 all; NASA/ESA/Hubble Hertitage Team(STScI/AIURA): 8br; NASA/Hubble
Heritage Team/STScI: 8cl; NASA/STScI: 8tl; Science Photo Library: 4/5bg (original), 5tr, 9tr, 9c, 18; Shutterstock: front cover, 2/3bg, 7bl, 13 all, 19 all, 22tr,
24bg; SOHO Project, NASA's Goddard Space Flight Center: 12br; ticktock picture archive: 6/7bg, 7tl, 10/11, 11tr, 12tl, 14, 15 all, 16, 17tr, 21bl, 14/15bg,
18/19bg, 22/23bg. Rocket drawing Dave Kowalski/ © Gareth Stevens, Inc.

Every effort has been made to trace the copyright holders for the photos used in this book. The publisher apologizes,
in advance, for any unintentional omissions and would be pleased to insert the appropriate acknowledgments in
any subsequent edition of this publication.

Printed in Canada

1 2 3 4 5 6 7 8 9 10 10 09 08 07 06

Contents

Words in the glossary are printed in **bold** the first time they appear in the text.

The Sun in the Solar System

Our Sun is a star. It is the center of our **solar system**. All of the planets, moons, **asteroids**, and other space objects **orbit** the Sun.

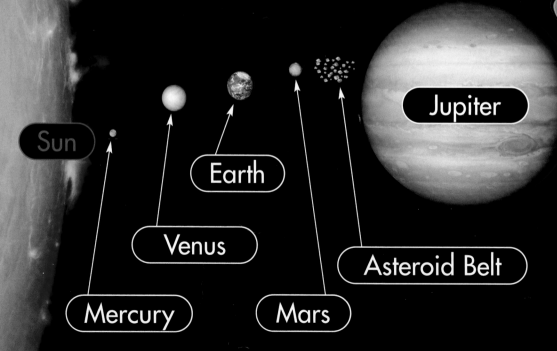

Sun

Mercury

Venus

Earth

Mars

Asteroid Belt

Jupiter

The Sun is the most important star in our sky. It is the closest star to Earth, and we see it during the day. Billions of other stars we see at night are all very, very far away.

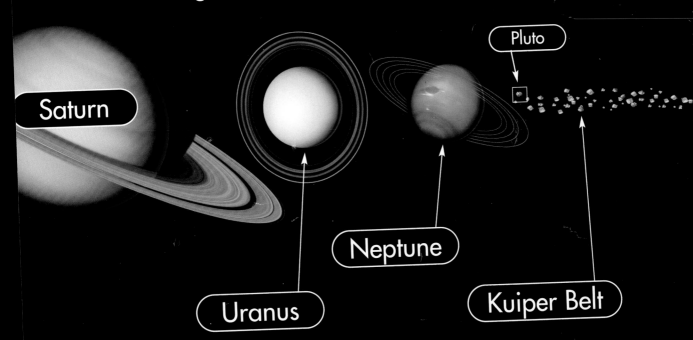

Saturn

Uranus

Neptune

Pluto

Kuiper Belt

Sun Facts

Like all stars, the Sun is a ball of exploding gases. The burning gases create heat and light. The Sun's heat and light reach Earth and all the other objects in the solar system.

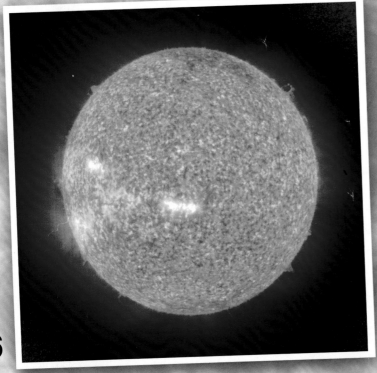

Our Sun is made of two gases, called **hydrogen** and **helium**. The Sun changes hydrogen into helium to make heat and light.

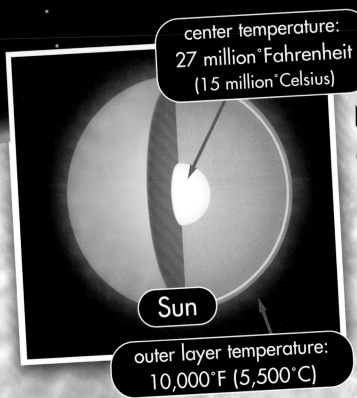

Sun

outer layer temperature:
10,000°F (5,500°C)

Nothing on Earth can compare to the heat of the Sun. The Sun has several layers of heat. The center temperature deep inside the Sun is the hottest.

The Sun is so hot because it is so big. It is many times larger than Earth. Next to the Sun, Earth looks like a tiny dot.

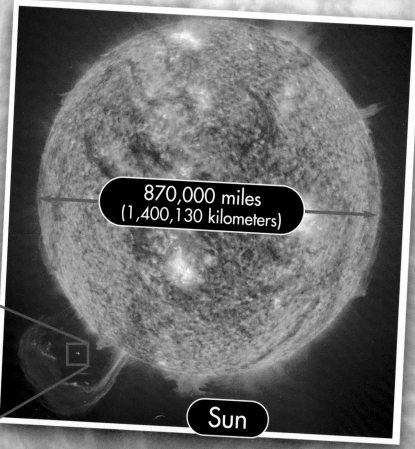

870,000 miles
(1,400,130 kilometers)

Sun

Earth

7,926 miles
(12,757 km)

7

The Birth of the Sun

Before the Sun was born, our solar system did not exist! The Sun's life began billions of years ago.

The birth of our Sun might have looked somewhat like the picture on the left.

A cloud of gases and dust began spinning. As it spun faster and faster, its center began to bulge.

As the bulge got bigger and spun faster, it got hotter and hotter. Hydrogen gas and helium gas began forming.

bulge

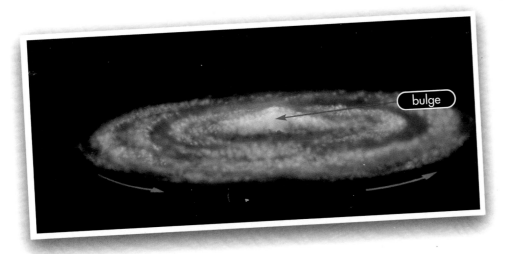

bulge

The very center of the bulge became the Sun. Planets and other objects in the solar system formed from the rest of the spinning disk.

The Sun's Life

The Sun is about five billion years old. But like people, plants, and animals, the Sun cannot live forever. Someday, it will die.

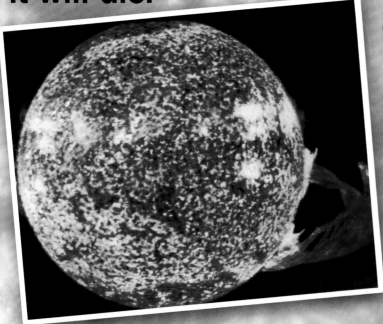

Our Sun is about halfway through its life. About half of its hydrogen gas has changed into helium gas.

It will take the Sun about another five billion years to use up all of its hydrogen gas.

The Sun will then grow until it becomes about one hundred times larger than it is now. It will become a type of star called a **red giant**.

red giant

Sun

Someday, our Sun will change into a red giant star and be hundreds of times larger.

white dwarf

After the Sun becomes a red giant, it will keep changing. All of its gases will start moving out into space and begin cooling. The Sun will then become a type of star called a **white dwarf** and cool for millions of years.

Sometimes, the Sun has dark spots on its outer layer. The dark spots are called **sunspots**.

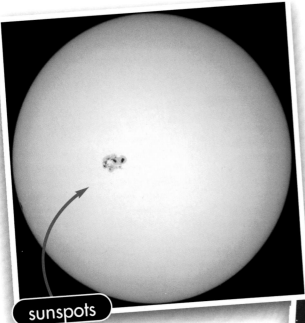

sunspots

Sunspots look dark because they are cooler than the rest of the Sun. Every eleven years, the Sun has more sunspots than usual.

solar flare

Some explosions on the Sun send extremely hot **particles** out into space. These are called **solar flares**.

12

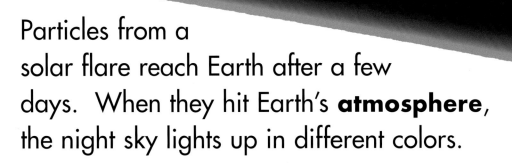

Particles from a
solar flare reach Earth after a few
days. When they hit Earth's **atmosphere**,
the night sky lights up in different colors.

These colors seem to
dance in the night sky.
We call the dancing
colored lights the
northern lights, or
the aurora borealis.

The aurora australis, or
southern lights, happen when
a solar flare reaches Earth's
southern atmosphere.

Eclipses

At times, the Moon's orbit takes it between Earth and the Sun. When this happens, the Moon blocks all or part of the Sun's light. This is called a solar **eclipse**.

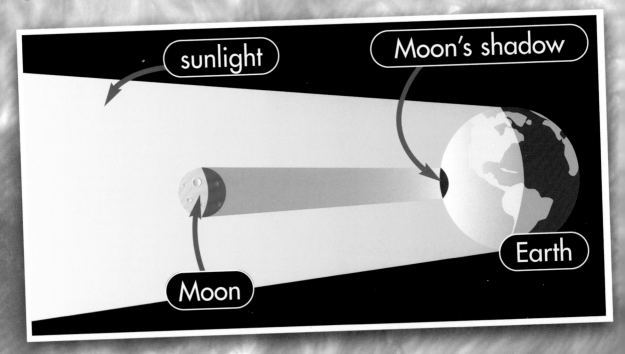

sunlight

Moon's shadow

Earth

Moon

As the Moon moves between Earth and the Sun, a shadow falls on Earth. For a few minutes, the Moon blocks out all of the Sun's light. This is called a total solar eclipse.

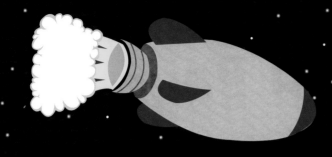

This picture shows a **partial** eclipse of the Sun. Only part of the Sun is covered as the Moon passes by.

Moon covering part of the Sun

Sun

Moon covering the Sun

glowing corona

We can only see the Sun's **corona** during a total solar eclipse. The corona is a ring of glowing gas around the Sun.

Winds and Rays

The Sun gives off more than heat and light. It also gives off all sorts of **rays**. Some of these rays are dangerous to life on Earth.

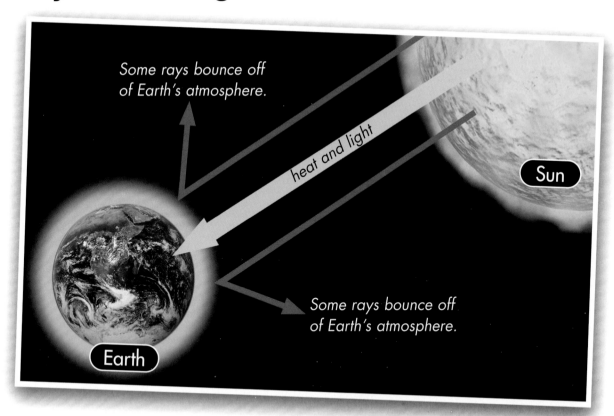

Some rays bounce off of Earth's atmosphere.

heat and light

Sun

Some rays bounce off of Earth's atmosphere.

Earth

The yellow arrow shows the Sun's heat and light reaching Earth. Red arrows show the Sun's dangerous rays. Earth's atmosphere makes some of the Sun's rays bounce back into space.

Another kind of ray leaves the Sun at very high speeds. This is called the solar wind. Most of the solar wind curves around Earth and goes on into space.

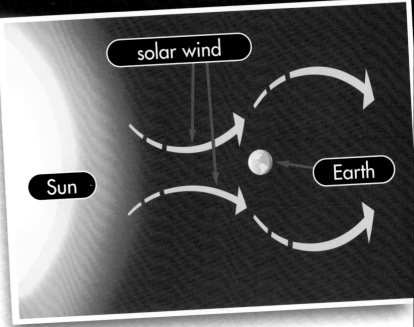

solar wind

Sun

Earth

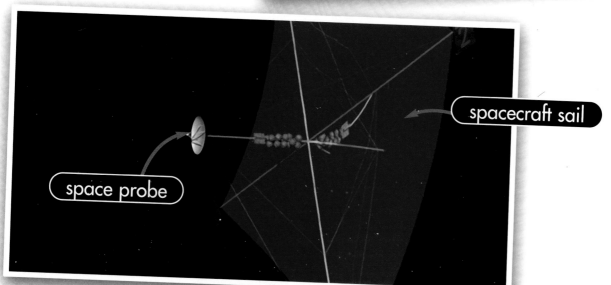

spacecraft sail

space probe

Some **astronomers** think the solar wind could push spacecraft along, like sailing ships in space!

17

What Can We See?

NEVER look at the Sun directly, with or without a telescope. The Sun will burn your eyes, and you could lose your sight.

telescope

Sun

image of the Sun

Early astronomers studied the Sun using a telescope and a piece of paper. They pointed the telescope toward the Sun. Instead of looking through the telescope, they held a piece of paper to catch the Sun's image.

Now, astronomers use special telescopes with **filters** to view the Sun safely from Earth.

Warning!
NEVER look directly at the Sun. It can blind you!

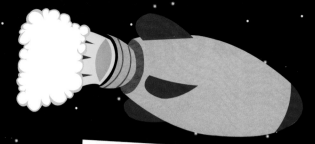

Humans, other animals, and plants all need sunlight to live and grow. The Sun's light lets us see colors during the day. At night, we see mostly black, white, and gray.

Too much sunlight can harm us. Our skin turns darker or even burns if we stay in the Sun too long. We must protect our skin with clothes, **sunscreen**, or shade.

19

The Sun in History

For thousands of years,
people believed the Sun was a god.
They knew the Sun could make their
crops grow or dry up their fields.
The Sun was important and powerful.

In ancient Egypt, people thought the Sun was
the king of the Gods. They named him "Ra."
Ra had a hawk's head and a human body.

He wore the Sun like a hat.

Ancient Greeks and Romans called their Sun god "Helios." They believed he crossed the sky in a flaming **chariot**.

In the Hindu religion, people have believed in a Sun god for thousands of years. He is called "Surya," and he rides a chariot with seven horses.

Missions to the Sun

Earth's atmosphere blocks out some of the Sun's rays. Astronomers use special spacecraft to study the different rays of the Sun.

The best way to study the Sun is from space. Some **space probes** orbit the Sun, while others can study the Sun from an obit around Earth.

Sun

satellite

Earth

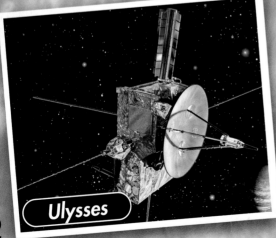

Ulysses

The *Ulysses* space probe was launched in 1990. It began orbiting and studying the Sun in 1994. *Ulysses's* third solar orbit began in November 2006.

Sun

SOHO

The *Solar and Heliospheric Observatory* (*SOHO*) space probe has studied the Sun since April 1996.

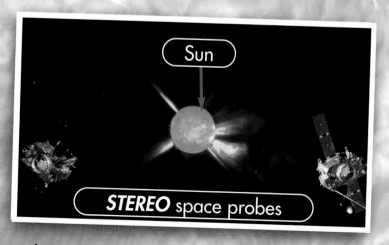

The *Solar Terrestrial Relations Observatory* (*STEREO*) mission reached Earth orbit in October 2006. *STEREO*'s two space probes will take 3-D pictures of solar activity.

Sun

STEREO space probes

Glossary

asteroids rocky objects that orbit the Sun. Most asteroids orbit the Sun between Mars and Jupiter.

astronomers scientists who study outer space, often using telescopes

atmosphere the gases that surround a planet, moon, or star

chariot a small cart that is pulled by horses

corona the glowing ring of solar gases seen only during a total eclipse

eclipse a blocking of light caused by a moon or planet

filters coverings for telescope lenses that block out some of the Sun's rays

helium gas a gas found on and made by the Sun

hydrogen gas a light gas found on the Sun

orbit the path that a planet or other object takes when traveling around the Sun, or the path a moon or satellite takes around a planet

partial something that is not complete

particles tiny amounts or very small pieces of matter

rays beams of light, heat, or particles

red giant a dying star that is slowly getting larger

solar having to do with the Sun

solar flares bursts of particles from the Sun that shoot out into space

solar system the Sun and everything that is in orbit around it

space probe a spacecraft sent from Earth to explore the solar system

sunspots cooler spots on the Sun's surface that look like dark freckles

sunscreen a spray or lotion that keeps the Sun's rays from harming skin

white dwarf a dying star that is slowly losing its gases to space

Index